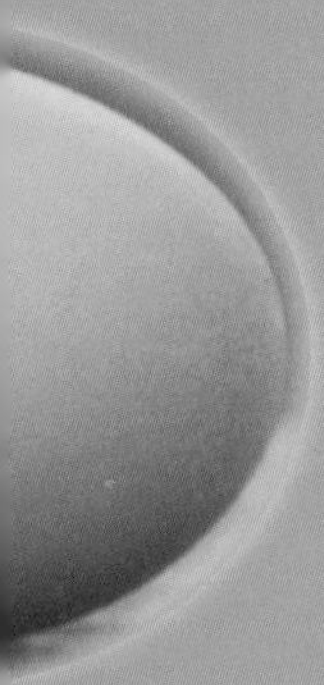

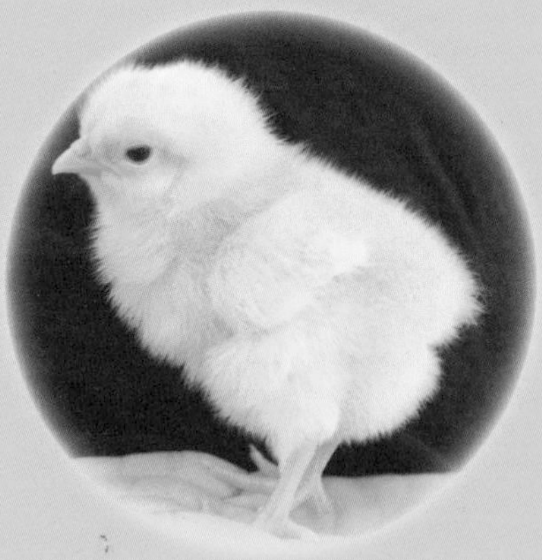

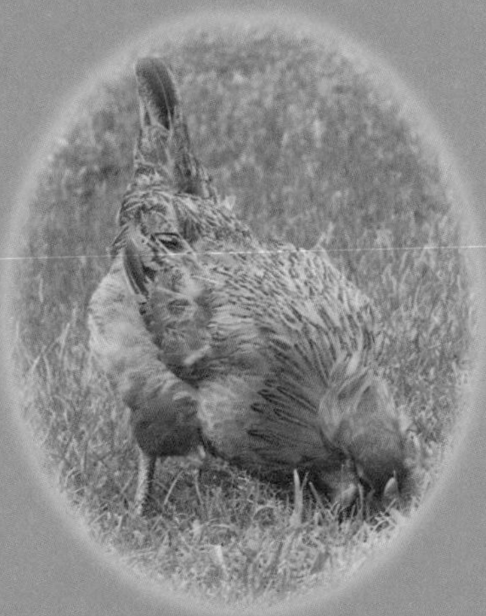

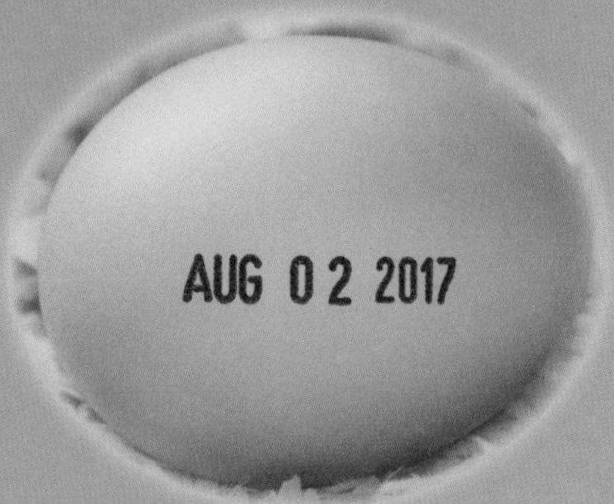

Young Chicken Farmers

Tips for Kids Raising Backyard Chickens

by Vickie Black

BEAVER'S
POND
PRESS

Dedicated to Brady and Hudson, my young chicken farmers. You fill my life and heart with joy. And to Jason, nothing's possible without you.

Thank you to Amalia, Luke, Tyler, Dylan, and Cody; the other young chicken farmers in my life who helped with photographs.

ISBN 978-1-59298-555-5

Library of Congress Catalog Number: 2012916819

Printed in the United States of America

First Printing: 2013

16 15 14 13   4 3 2 1

Photography by Vickie Black
Edited by Lily Coyle
Book design by Sara Weingartner

Beaver's Pond Press, Inc.
7108 Ohms Lane
Edina, MN 55439-2129
(952) 829-8818
www.BeaversPondPress.com

BEAVER'S
POND
PRESS

To order, visit www.BeaversPondBooks.com or call 1-800-901-3480.
Reseller discounts available.

www.beaverspondpress.com

Where do eggs come from? [Chickens, of course!]

But where do chickens come from? [Eggs, of course!]

Which one came first? [That's a completely different story.]

Can you believe I used to fit inside that egg?

No matter which came first, there's a lot to think about before getting chickens.

So many choices!

Chickens come in many different breeds and varieties. They all start out as adorable fluffy chicks, but grow up to look and act differently. Some breeds are friendlier and make better pets than others. Some are happy living in a **coop**, while others like to **free range**. Some lay more eggs than others. If you want to be a **young chicken farmer**, learn about different breeds before making your decision.

You don't need a farm to be a chicken farmer, but before you buy chickens...

- Check the zoning laws where you live. Not all cities allow backyard chickens, and some have restrictions.
- Think about how much space you have and where they will live.
- Happy chickens live in **flocks**. Be sure you have enough room for at least three chickens.
- Decide if you have time to do chicken chores.

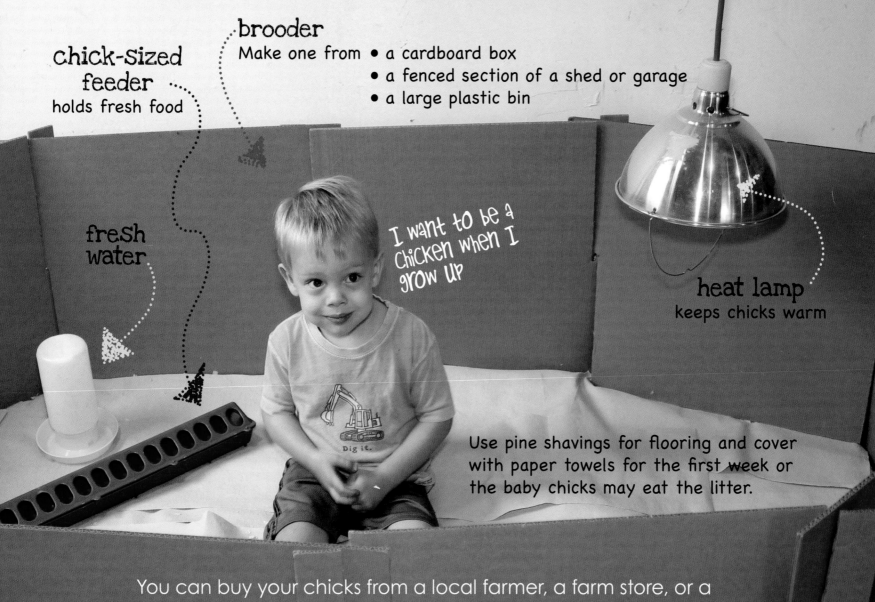

chick-sized feeder holds fresh food

brooder
Make one from
- a cardboard box
- a fenced section of a shed or garage
- a large plastic bin

I want to be a chicken when I grow up

fresh water

heat lamp keeps chicks warm

Use pine shavings for flooring and cover with paper towels for the first week or the baby chicks may eat the litter.

Dig it.

You can buy your chicks from a local farmer, a farm store, or a hatchery. A **chicken hatchery** is a place where eggs are hatched, and chicks are shipped to families all over the country. While you wait for the chicks to arrive, you can get the **brooder** ready. A brooder is a safe, warm place for the chicks to grow until they have all of their feathers—usually four to six weeks.

Welcome home, little chicks!

wood shavings

air holes

The box is taped to secure the lid so no chicks escape.

If you order chicks from a hatchery, they'll be shipped through the mail when they're one day old. Someone from the post office will call you when they arrive so you can pick them up. Everyone loves getting packages in the mail, but few things are more exciting than a box of baby chicks!

When you get them home, remove the chicks, one by one, from their box. Carefully dip each chick's beak in water to help it start drinking. Then release it into the warm brooder. Once all the chicks are drinking, you can add special chick food using a chick-sized feeder.

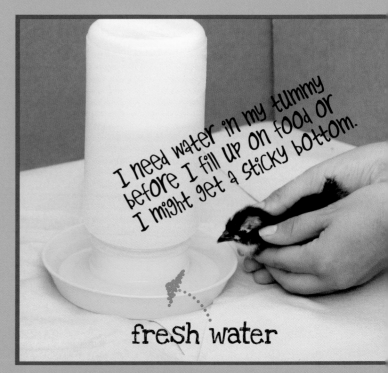

I need water in my tummy before I fill up on food or I might get a sticky bottom.

fresh water

Shh... it's naptime.

When the chicks settle down from the transition to their new home, they'll rest. It has been a big day! They'll nap often while they're small, just like you did when you were a baby. Sometimes they'll nap in your lap if you're quiet and gentle.

You can buy chick food, called starter ration, at a farm store, feed store, or even online!

Refer to a book like *Storey's Guide to Raising Chickens* if your chicks have sticky bottoms or show other signs of sickness.

Always be very careful when handling baby chicks. When you pick up a chick, it's best to move close slowly from the side. You can also talk or sing so your chicks know you're coming.

If anyone has ever snuck up behind you and said, "Boo" you know what it's like to be startled. Chicks are easily frightened, so the best way to approach them is when they can see you.

Please don't **squeeze** me!

Hold baby chicks gently with both hands. When you're ready to let the chick go, open your hands on the ground or the bottom of the brooder so the chick can walk away and not fall.

Sharing is almost always a good idea, but you don't want to share germs with your chicks. That's why you should *always* wash your hands with soap and water before and after handling your chicks.

Peep!

Peep! Peep!

Egg-citing fact:

Keeping the brooder clean and dry is a great way to keep your chicks healthy and happy.

Have you ever heard a chicken talk? It's not as silly as it sounds, but chicks don't use words. They'll tell you if they're too cold by huddling on top of each other. If they're too hot they'll gather along the edges of the brooder. When they're happy, they explore the brooder singing, **"Peep, peep, peep."**

Sometimes new experiences are scary. In the beginning, chicks huddle in a heap and peep, peep, peep during lights out.

Watch them closely. When chicks huddle they can smother the ones on the bottom of the pile.

Have you ever been **afraid** of the dark? You're not alone. Chicks are too! You can help your chicks practice getting used to the dark by turning out the lights for a short time each day. Pick the warmest part of the day so your chicks don't get cold.

9

Brooder escape!

As chicks get stronger and grow feathers on their wings, they can fly out of the brooder. Unfortunately, they usually won't fly back in. Covering the brooder with a screen or chicken wire will prevent chicks from escaping and getting lost or hurt.

Boy or girl?

- Female chicks are called **pullets**. When they grow up they're called **hens**.

- Male chicks are called **cockerels**. When they grow up they're called **roosters**.

- Hens lay eggs.

- Roosters crow:

"Cock-a-doodle-doo!"

Egg-citing fact:

When ordering chicks, you can get:
- pullets
- cockerels
- straight run (mix of both)

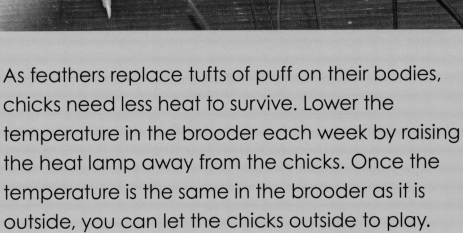

As feathers replace tufts of puff on their bodies, chicks need less heat to survive. Lower the temperature in the brooder each week by raising the heat lamp away from the chicks. Once the temperature is the same in the brooder as it is outside, you can let the chicks outside to play.

More about coops

- A coop should be designed to keep chickens safe from **predators**. A weasel only needs a one-inch hole to get in the coop and harm the chickens.

- Keep the chicks penned for at least two weeks so they learn that the coop is their home.

Coop ramp

When the temperature is right and the chicks are covered with feathers, they can move to their permanent home, called a **coop**, in the yard. A coop usually has an indoor enclosure and a fenced area so the chickens can go outside.

The scoop on the coops...

Nighty-night!

Coops need plenty of roosting space. Chickens don't sleep lying down like you do. They rest and sleep close to each other on a roost.

A roost can be made from a board, a sturdy branch, or an old ladder. Remove splinters so the chickens' feet don't get injured.

roost

They come in all shapes and sizes!

watch out for predators!

Keep your chickens safe with a secure coop, and watch for these animals when your chickens are out:

Rats

Minks

Hawks

Dogs

Foxes

Weasels

Cats

Coyotes

Raccoons

Skunks

You exercise to keep your body healthy, and so should your chickens. When it's safe, you can release your flock from their coop to range in the yard. Chickens are expert explorers! They'll eat grass, bugs, worms, and even your vegetable garden if they have the chance. When they've had enough fun, chickens usually go back to their coop on their own.

Vine-ripened tomatoes are my favorite treat!

15

C-o-m-e and get it!

A balanced diet is good for both you and your chickens. Chickens need protein, vitamins, and minerals, which they will get from their feed. They'll cackle with delight when you feed them **scratch** and other healthy snacks.

Chickens love leftovers!

Try sharing your:

- strawberry tops
- melon rinds
- lettuce, spinach, sprouts
- even your cooked eggs!

Here Chick, Chick, Chick

As your chicks develop and grow, they need different food, just like you do! Check with a feed store or online to see what type of food your flock needs. If your flock eats scratch and other grains, they'll also need **grit** to help them digest their unchewed food. Chickens can't chew, because they don't have teeth!

scratch
made from grains and is tossed on the ground or fed from the hand.

grit
made from sand, gravel, or small stones and is given separately.

Silly things chickens do.

Hey that's my toe!

Is that a worm?

Chickens peck at the ground with their beaks when they are looking for food. They may also peck at objects they're afraid of or curious about. They scratch their feet on the ground when they're looking for food, like they're hunting for buried treasure.

Watch out for pecking!

If you're sitting close to or holding your chickens, don't be surprised if they peck at a hair ribbon, beads on your shirt, or freckles on your skin. Be careful—even your eyelashes might be tempting for a curious chicken.

18

Scrub-a-dub-dub... 3 in a tub!

Ba-gok! Give me some room please!

Have you ever taken a bath in dirt? Does it sound like fun? Chickens take dust baths by rolling in dirt and fluffing it through their feathers. This helps them stay cool when it's hot and it keeps their feathers clean.

To make a dust bath:

Put dirt in the coop, on the ground, or in a sturdy container.

You can teach a chicken!

Chickens learn to associate a reward with the farmer's call.

Here chick, chick, chick

Yum!

Run, they have treats!

Just like your friends, chickens all have different personalities. While some breeds are more comfortable with people than others are, you may be able to train your chickens to come when you call. This is helpful if you need to get chickens back in their coop when they're playing in the yard.

Fun toys for chickens!

- a tin pie plate nailed to the coop wall
- a wire ball stuffed with apples or lettuce
- a treat filled ball with holes on either end
- a mirror

That's my truck

Can I play too?

Chickens are curious and can easily get bored in their coop. When chickens are bored they may peck at each other. You can share your toys, or find special toys that only chickens love. Use your imagination, what can they peck at?

compost
Chicken poop works wonders in your **compost bin**!

If you are a young chicken farmer, you have chores to do every day because healthy, happy chickens need your attention. After all, there are feeders to fill and there is poop to scoop!

Everybody, do your share!

Chicken Chores

1 Give them fresh food and water every day.

2 Collect eggs every day.

3 Clean out dirty bedding and replace it with fresh bedding every week or two.

4 Talk to them and give them toys to play with.

5 When it's safe, let them out of the coop to play in the yard.

The moment all chicken farmers wait for finally arrives when the females are about six months old. The hens start laying eggs! The first eggs are often small and chickens could lay them just about anywhere. If you suspect your chickens are laying eggs in the yard while they are out and about, grab a basket and let the egg hunt begin!

Look, there's an egg!

What about roosters?

- You don't need a rooster to get eggs. Hens will lay eggs without a rooster around.
- You do need a rooster if you want fertilized eggs that will hatch into baby chicks.
- You do need a rooster if you want an alarm clock that sings "Cock-a-doodle-doo!"

23

Yeah!
It is a
good one.

If you find an egg and you're not sure how long it's been where you found it, conduct an experiment to see if it's fresh. Put the egg in a glass of water. If it sinks, it's good; if it floats, pick something else for breakfast...

How do you know if a chicken laid an egg?
If you're listening closely,
you may hear her cackle.
Maybe that's her way of saying,
"I did it!"

Once they have some practice, each hen will start laying one to five eggs per week in the nesting box. A nesting box is an area in the coop that will provide the hens a clean, dry, dark place to lay their eggs.

Egg-citing facts:
- The color of the egg depends on the breed of chicken.
- Chicken eggs can be white, brown, green, or blue.

Train your hen!
You can put golf balls in the nest to encourage hens to lay eggs there, instead of the yard.

The first one to the fence

With an unbroken egg wins!

●●●●●

Most hens will lay for a few years. What will you do with all of those eggs? Don't worry, there's no limit to the possibilities when you use your imagination. Eggs taste yummy and give your body protein to make you strong.

Many ways to use eggs:

- Have an egg-and-spoon race with your friends
- Put them in recipes for baking
- Scramble them for breakfast
- Dye them for Easter

Glossary

Brooder – A warm, enclosed area where baby chicks live until they are ready to move outside.

Coop – A cage where adult chickens live.

Chicken hatchery – A place where eggs are hatched and the baby chicks are sent to farms and families all over the United States.

Compost bin – A place to put garden clippings, chicken poop, soiled coop litter, and other organic matter where it can break down. Compost is an excellent garden fertilizer.

Flock – Several chickens that live together.

Free range – Chickens that are not confined and eat naturally.

Grit – Gravel or small stones that chickens eat to help them digest their food.

Heat lamp – A special lamp used to heat a brooder to keep baby chicks warm.

Hen – A female chicken. Female baby chicks are called "pullets" until they are about a year old.

Nesting box – An area in the coop where chickens go to lay their eggs.

Predator – An animal that hunts other animals (like chickens) and harms them or kills them.

Roost – An elevated piece of wood that chickens sit on while they sleep or rest.

Rooster – A male chicken. Male baby chicks are called "cockerels" until they are about a year old.

Scratch – 1) A mixture of corn and grains used for treats. 2) When chickens toss dirt or grass with their feet to uncover food to eat.

Straight run – When male and female chicks ordered from a hatchery are mixed together.

Young chicken farmer – A child who helps take care of chickens.

Pick Your Chicken

There are many resources to help you decide the right breed of chicken for you. Here are a few:

- The "breed selection tool" at www.mypetchicken.com
- *Storey's Illustrated Guide to Poultry Breeds* by Gail Damerow; Storey Publishing, LLC
- *The Illustrated Guide to Chickens: How to Choose Them, How to Keep Them* by Celia Lewis; Skyhorse Publishing

comb

Did you know?

Adult chickens have a comb and wattles that wiggle when they walk.

wattle

About the Author

Vickie Black is a wife, mother, and proud backyard chicken farmer. A resident of MN, she has a bachelor's of science, a master's of education, and works as a marketing consultant. The family got their inspiration for raising chickens while visiting a local pumpkin patch that had a small flock. Her husband Jason built their coop in the garage over the winter, with the help of their two boys, Brady and Hudson. The family loves the entertainment and fresh eggs that the chickens provide.